Sensitive to Temperature

Serena Alagappan

NEW**POETS**LIST

the poetry business

Published 2023 by
New Poets List
The Poetry Business
Campo House,
54 Campo Lane,
Sheffield S1 2EG

ISBN 978-1-914914-47-8
eBook ISBN 978-1-914914-48-5
Typeset by Utter
Cover image: Luke Stackpole on Unsplash
Printed by Biddles Books

Smith|Doorstop Books are a member of Inpress:
www.inpressbooks.co.uk

Distributed by NBN International, 1 Deltic Avenue,
Rooksley, Milton Keynes MK13 8LD

The Poetry Business gratefully acknowledges
the support of Arts Council England.

Supported by
**ARTS COUNCIL
ENGLAND**

Contents

slipface

gazing up at a long shallow angle of loose sand recalls
the typical dread: *if I reach out, will you make*
time for me?

the steep lee size of those aeolian landforms involves erosion:
what is left besides deflation, desert, and pavement?

there exist geological agents, such as rivers, glaciers, and waves, water –
really – who offer sediment. among these transformations comes

has the moment passed? sun radiates off the slipface, and longing in its breath, I
shake my head toward the dune. *no*, I say. *the moment's*
never passed with you.

The Sky Has a Body

The sky has a body – it blushes, coughs

with smoke, folds under atmospheric

pressure, warms pink, goes cold and quiet,

runs a fever, crowds with unwanted visitors,

expels birds like a throat swallows stones,

like a stomach stills a swarm of butterflies.

The sky wheezes with its wind, loses its

breath, belches thunder, heart beats shocks

of electricity and weeps from every pore

when it's hurting.

Aurora

Rory would bleed   so pretty like morning   but in a season

where light leaks rare, where   light is green,

marking a birth, or all that's pure

Rory smiles cause she's   fragile   but   icy too

These days   it's hard to   remember how

good a gash   in the sky feels   thawed

across   one's view   or losing track

of whose fingers belong to whom

Even more difficult   to recall   what was

beautiful without   witness

I think ignorance is   both a   blessing and a curse

Everything   became

slippery   confusing   after the first

Clockwork

A placebo is basically a metaphor:
still rigorous and true for the body.
Smells like summer and a bag between
us, a black tote eating sun never mind
the blue sky, weeks left, or leather
cushions our knees dropped into.
We like each other's eyes.

The eyes recalibrate as a result
of experience – meaning
everything we see can shrink
or magnify, meaning, sight is plastic.
We blink and the world rearranges.
We blink and it remains unchanged.

Just looking: sideways at a brick wall,
across the street at a bus, down at the
grass and its fruit flies, toward the floor,
pretending to be shy, or at the ceiling
before you bite, deciding a view is
beautiful – those are indiscernibly
small and precise recalibrations.

The earth does this too, tilts on
its axis, desires heat and light.
One orbit, which lasts 405,000 years,
helps geologists measure planetary
dynamics. Sedimentary records etch
their evidence in rock. That's how certain
a recalibration is, as certain as the globe
warming, fake medicine, false starts, real healing.

White Bows

You are too focused on the clutter of trailers
where purple towels sag
and hiccup in wind. I follow you around
with a disposable from the corner store.

You click your camera
after ten minutes of set-
ting up a scene. The square
shadow from one mobile
home covers you entirely till
you step outside to roll
someone's football into
the frame.

I try to enjoy watching you wait –
for clouds to spool over the sun,
which every minute blazes hotter. Your lens
gauze for the water slide's burn, a glare
I would've passed without glancing.

I stare at the ocean, which every hour rises
higher, stare at its crowd of wind turbines:
steel devices spin like waving hands,
          boomerang between
hello and goodbye, a resoundingly neutral
greeting, white bows in cerulean hair,
already a wet memory.

Despite Papa's unchewed sugar beard, one
vertigoless trip to a fair, and absolutely zero
promises to stay, the pier spits me out unscathed.
Make me a drink of water from humid air.

The Body Keeps the Score

After Bessel van der Kolk

The rock drags itself – no it is tugged, by
the wind and the softening winter pond,
a bowl depressing like a suncup, wound
wider than it is deep. Sailing
stones, the rocks that chart brushstrokes in sand,

are designed to leave their mark: veins in deserts
won't be wiped clean by the joy of any
far-off splashing. There's no threat here, no slosh
or stupor. It's dry. Stick a fist in the

earth and find dust on your palms. The past you
can't remember is the future you
can't imagine: filth and crisis. Beg it

away. Thin floating ice panels break up
on sunny days. Then the stones catapult –

slowly – up to five meters per minute,
they plod on. Sometimes the paths in the sand

slog, non-linear like ribbons of salt-
water on a flushed face, like healing or

forgetting. Tell the rock to stop. (It won't).

Leisureland

No longer played, the
game is called cosmic crane.
It's an abandoned arcade,
and this booth sports
a painted rocket,
tearing toward your
camera. Yoda, Spiderman
and Peter Rabbit droop,
hung on the gate in
front of a mirror.
Settled in the sea
of plastic hollow balls lies
a unicorn, stuffed
cadaver, pupils bulging, on
its side, like a valley
sleeper with bullet wounds.
Magic horse relaxed
and haunting. BIG PRIZES
BIG PRIZES repeat twice
in block letters – fists
thumping glass, foggy from
small hot mouths, vending
machine like Christmas
morning, and on the right,
a desperate whack-a-mole,
every animal skull
a future, rising like a fig,
evading its own shadow,
how a groundhog's cloudy
ceiling cries Spring.

After the Mushroom at the End of the World

These, remedial gestures: how
a spinning bulk of garbage in
the sea becomes a Holy Vortex
for a plastic bag's vagrancy,

how landfill picking transforms
for garden-artists: pluck, prune,
and glean like you're foraging
treasure on behalf of trash,

how after nuclear disaster,
mushrooms grow on reactor walls,
harnessing radiation like purple
alliums photosynthesize light,

happy globes bursting, these
flowers can nurture budding
stars in climates on the drier side,
drought-tolerant, they'll keep alive.

I read once, that there's a kind
of love that doesn't extend itself
both ways between two people
equally because it doesn't have to.

When air explodes hot and buoyant,
it bubbles and expands, waltzes with
open legs and a rising skirt, condensing
debris, sucking energy from decay.

What's left at the end of the world,
besides lichen, missile clouds blocking
the sun, and a harvest for two that
can only be tilled by one?

Author's Note: The fifth stanza references the end of Carl Phillips' poem "If You Go Away" and the title is inspired by Anna Tsing's *The Mushroom at the End of the World*.

Slugs in a Storm

from inside,   water torrents sound like fire;
          but a roommate is just home, drenched and gleam-

ing. there's a fresh onslaught of drops when you
          crank the window to exhale smoke from a

marble bowl. First-ever flash flood warning
          in New York. Of course you're here, eyes stretched, laugh

clipped, bright,   skin like mine. Me on the bed, you
          on the   floor.   We watch videos to pass the storm.

I remember what your mother said: once,
          you were a baby, mixing up words, and

bumping into things. I didn't believe
          her. I don't believe you when you say slugs

construct a rope when they fuck. But footage
          shows mucus bodies intertwine on string,

suspended from a branch, shivering mid-
          air. Their mutual cord   tunnels like a

column of twisting wind that in films tastes
          cars then hurls them back. tornados can come

soft too: one hungry kiss, your chances stacked.

Holy

Holy those colors in rain
after drought, a puddled vow,
iris damp and aching.

Holy the indigo aura
that casts doubt on a landscape's
verity. Fog or foam, snow
caps or sea?

Holy the difference between
solid and liquid – this thin: a
cloud thrums, only temporarily
pregnant.

Holy how time morphs
between shores,
how when suspended
in ice, petals burn to touch.

Holy their will to wither,
unholy their right to lie.

Holy to be mummified.

Holy atmosphere of glass,
shattered by the unjaded.

Holy temple on the beach,
which the tsunami passed.

Holy Hanuman, monkey-headed
deity turning winds in his hands.
Holy statue, draped in marigolds,
tearing open its chest.

Holy stars shrill in the sky.

Holy the potato
hauled out of the soil.
Holy the hairthin seed
of the potato plant.

Holy the volcano, and
the ones spared
from the volcano,
and the volcano's fertile sand.

Tiffin

After The Lunchbox (2013)

Tiffin clangs like bells,
collapses as it climbs,
tiffin holds okra, paneer,
sambar, and lemon rice.
Tiffin holds notes,
scrawled at lunchtime
while chewing. Tiffin
grows like a womb
bears a promise, a
later date and time.
Tiffin packs extra pride
with hurt feelings –
clipped spice – but a swirl
of cream if tasted with
two fingers. Tiffin
takes its time unpacking
even if the food goes cold.
Empty tiffin isn't the
finale you think. When
a container contains
negative space, there is
no longer an ending.
There is only an
invitation.

shop local

the stone pine is local, but a blueberry
plant sprouts rampant: the wife takes
to it with shears; she doesn't mind the bees.

her smash of avocado isn't local,
but it's heaping with feta
in a square city with prime dimensions.

she drinks jitterless CBD infused
cold brew, bred on campus, by two buddies
in a frat house.

before the tech bubble, she needed maps.
her dot didn't move,
only guidebook pages in sweaty hands.

in this nuptial story, the camera
zooms in on the curtain, its shadow, two
empty bottles of flat, oaky vino,

then the woman, who identifies as
married, flinching, asking to be alone,
a single tear on a tightrope.

How Dark the Beginning

After Maggie Smith

The charcoal wasn't burning so the food
was raw. Sky ruddy. You were snacking on
halloumi, taking pictures of your ex

as she spun in a long green dress. No one
has ever bent back in the grass before
me like that, laughing with an audience

of gnats, and a dog who plunged into the
marsh, hunting a bird who'd forgotten how
to fly. That night, I pulled a sheet around

my body and realized that my tee-
shirt mapped a constellation of stars, that
cloth territory could glow in the dark.

Red Moon

You said *God is this close*, then slapped your
palm across your eyes. Your hand was not only
too close to see, but also preventing your sight.
Metaphors aren't always so neat.

Imagining your pain seven years ago would have
sunk me. Then, like an ant within a scalloped
leaf, nestled between bits of silt and twig,
I curled in my closet, like you did when your heart
broke, which you told me in a poem.

Signs of persistence: a wedding dress made of
bandages, wisdom teeth budding despite war, and
an army nurse who saved two soldiers on opposing sides.
Her explanation: there is not one heart for love and
one for hatred. There is only one heart for both.

Facts I know because my parents told me:
prayer may not pour water on parched fields
but it can nourish a dry soul, there is pleasure in
falling at God's feet, time is precious, look forward,
say please, and even more, pray thank you.

We have spun out and wandered back, but all I
think of now is the night in stained glass, the same
night we stared at a red moon from the roof of a
laboratory, the various rooves climbing, and the
certainty with which I know you will recover is the
certainty with which I remember: sharp, exploding, sure.

even now, assembling

even now, this dreamscape is assembling,
even as the screws twist left. the only
thing we built together is unfinished:

the dresser's cardboard spine pinned, but drawers on
the floor, severed panels I step over
in the dark. noting each detail, I watched

you count each nail. because I'm impatient,
I'll leave it this way – gaping – with sunrise
seeping through my window shades. I want to

wake with a stutter or a slap. I no
longer believe in things coming ready-
made. I expect to need a hammer. when I've

slept enough, I'll pluck a costume off its
hanger, and when I spin in that pretty
dress, it'll be like screws are in my feet.

Nostalgia Architects

So many memorials sigh with water:
water plunging down into a gaping
crevice, the negative space of building,
water falling thunderous, or rippling noiseless,
water running backward on a table, parting
to reveal martyrs and heroes, when touched.

So many memorials nurture trees:
baby Callery pears, brought as saplings,
not seeds. Eight yellowwoods planted
in 1993 for the eight women etched
into the wall. Cherry blossoms,
which speckle a green space pink.

So many memorials are ordered by
age, date, home, hobby, friends,
family, neighbors, workplace, or alphabet.
With too much text to see or read,
I imagine the storm of a thousand paper cranes.
Chasing hundreds of words with my fingers,
I keep searching for your name.

Forest Fire from Far Away

red   hole
in the sky:
scalding
coal in the
palm.

(mythologized
matchsticks)

that man held
fire: his scar proof
of courage. but the
earth boasts no
injury. is pride only
bred from wounds
self-inflicted?

forest burns
for miles,
from the valley,
from the shore,
atop that mountain:
orange sparks
like a giddy star.

(aestheticized,
anthropomorphized)

alight from the inside.
sore haze, bloodshot
sea: what will
the earth bear
for this brutality?

The Beginning of the Thames

A river's   mouth throats into the ocean. Where then
does it start?   I imagined something grand, as I had
for about five   years. A mountain crush into liquid
matter, blue silk in a   secret garden, something magic
pooling before the surge   that clefts the city. I'd been
waiting for a jarred metre, like   a dam clogs water.
I found kicked up mud instead   grass torn and mixed
with hay, a bit underfed, the water   appeared from
nowhere, perhaps a spring beneath   the   earth, you
guessed. Aloud, as if to ensure a record   unusual warmth
for a February morning, rolls of soil   like dirt waves, a soft
pony pausing to chew as it wobbled   around a pasture.
No one was there to bear witness   but it started as a
dribble, then further down   turned into a stream.
Trees, bared by cold   stood naked, shivering, and
an orange hole   in the sky singed between them.
Color above   the creek (for it can only, in Cirencester,
be called a creek)   hovered, the way time loves its
arbitrary signs   half a decade ago, almost to the day,
I first had sex   I felt as a river might when it becomes
subsumed in salt   as if someone had died. Nothing
reminds you   of ending more than recalling another
beginning   Now this one foray into the forest has
arresting   random meaning. Cyclical markers buoy me.
Like when I   dreamed of a great aunt I'd never met
on her would-be   hundredth birthday, and thought
myself a mystic   I've been called neurotic, crazy,
a Jewish girl with   Catholic sensibilities (all in the same
breath), but if a river   can begin this clear, then low
hours can climb their way   out new mouths. Seaweed storm
below surface glass permits a green   reflection   green, as in
newly alive, chlorophyll- innocence. Thames has not   met the
city yet. Isn't it nice to think she won't, to pretend and to forget?

Sensitive to Temperature

Frost at high altitudes in the Atacama Desert reaps snow stuck so tight
flakes look like bones, or like pilgrims stooped in worship, when their chins
grind their sternums and their eyes humor sporadic peeks skyward.

*

Penitentes get their name in the Dry Andes from the converts who,
inconsolable, buckle from their feet. The jagged promise made by
crowding glacial blades might likewise move you to your knees.

*

Spires under a night sky, glinting like the stars that stake their claim in
darkness, still won't melt when licked by sun if they're high enough. Elderly
icicles, reversed in their rising, also stand fifty feet tall on a satellite of Jupiter.

*

Those frigid mountain vanes are a just a few hundred million miles
away. They live close too: in me and you, sensitive to temperature,
frozen in numb rupture.

Let's Catch Up Soon

You'd like to ventriloquize
that leaf, or the veins bulging
inside it, cul-de-sac
of the clementine wedge,
bumpy with seeds (one more
dead end street). Pulp thick
with fruit hair, tree blood,
lavender honey, syrup
boiled and tapped, one more
sweet thing to extract.

Waiting for fruits to soften
is waiting for a friend
with whom it's been a long
time since you've spoken.

You'd like to ventriloquize
the rot, the fur, the bowl going
bad, the brown parts of the
peach, the mush of berries, apple
skin wrinkling, pieces of flesh re-
consumed by soil. It's true,
you speak for muck, but time
is still mould: hold
your breath, (deceptive
cadence), it grows.

Acknowledgements

Thank you to my eighth grade English teacher, Jordie Kattan, for showing me an essay she'd written in college called 'Scar Tissue.' A phrase from that essay became this chapbook's title.

Thank you to my editor, Suzannah Evans, and my poetry workshop instructors, Daljit Nagra, Tracy K. Smith, and Rachael Allen, for their feedback and inspiration.

Thank you to the *Cambridge Review of Books* for publishing 'The Sky Has a Body.'

Thank you to *Stand Magazine* for publishing 'Clockwork.'

Thank you to *Bear Review* for publishing early versions of 'The Body Keeps the Score' and 'Sensitive to Temperature.'

Thank you to *petrichor magazine* for publishing an early version of 'Leisureland.'

Thank you to the *Colorado Review* for publishing 'After the Mushroom at the End of the World,' and thank you to the Ginkgo Prize in Ecopoetry for anthologizing it.

Thank you to the environmental zine *Earthen* for publishing 'Slugs in a Storm.'

Thank you to *Porridge Magazine* for publishing 'Tiffin.'

Thank you to the *London Magazine* for publishing 'shop local.'

Thank you to *Postscript Magazine* for publishing 'Red Moon.'

Thank you to the *Madras Courier* for publishing 'Forest Fire from Far Away.'